E 6-95

Elizabeth Rogers

Hir Virginall Booke

Elizabeth Rogers Hir Virginall Booke

112 CHOICE PIECES FOR HARPSICHORD BY BYRD, GIBBONS, LAWES, AND OTHERS

Editing and Calligraphy by

CHARLES J. F. COFONE

SECOND, REVISED EDITION

DOVER PUBLICATIONS, INC.

NEW YORK

Published in Canada by General Publishing Company, Ltd.,
30 Lesmill Road, Don Mills, Toronto, Ontario.
Published in the United Kingdom by Constable and Company, Ltd.,
10 Orange Street, London WC2H 7EG.

This is the second, revised edition, 1982, of the work originally published
by Dover Publications, Inc., in 1975.

International Standard Book Number: 0-486-23138-0
Library of Congress Catalog Card Number: 73-94344
Manufactured in the United States of America

Dover Publications, Inc.
180 Varick Street
New York, N.Y. 10014

To my Mother and Father
and Carol and Evie

Acknowledgments I would like to thank all of those people who were of both spiritual and corporal assistance to me during the preparation of this edition, especially the following.

First, I would like to thank the Trustees of the British Museum and the Photographic Department of the British Museum for their reproductions of the original manuscript and the permission to reproduce them. A special note of thanks to Mr. Hugh Cobbe, Assistant Keeper of Manuscripts, for his invaluable assistance and remarks regarding the history of the manuscript.

I would also like to thank Clarence Strowbridge and Stanley Appelbaum for all of their assistance, advice and concern in the preparation of this book.

An extra special note of thanks to Gella and Thanos Skouras for their hospitality during my stay in London.

Special thanks to Bernard Rubin and Barbara Sabbath for their spiritual, gastronomic and automotive companionship during my stay in Italy.

E vorrei ringraziare specialmente i miei cari amici, Augusto e Mary Alice De Flaviis Sorriso, per la loro amicizia, gentilezza ed ospitalità durante il mio soggiorno a Firenze.

And a very special heartfelt thanks to an anonymous friend for making this project as pleasant at its outset as could possibly have been desired.

Note to the Second Edition A grateful thank you to Robert Gutchen for his time, care and notes on the subject of the political history of the age.

And finally I would like to thank Dr. Howard Ferguson for his suggestions, corrections and impeccable care in reading and annotating this transcription.

C. J. C.

Contents

CONTENTS

Introduction

HISTORY OF
THE MANUSCRIPT

Elizabeth Rogers hir virginall booke is a manuscript commonplace-book in the collection of the British Museum, London, where it is catalogued as Additional Manuscript 10337. It was purchased by the Museum on Wednesday, 17 February 1836, for ten shillings, at the sale of the extensive library of the well-known nineteenth-century bibliophile and collector, Richard Heber. The manuscript has remained since that time in the British Museum. It was rebound in 1949, using part of the original covers.

The volume of the catalogue of the sale containing reference to the manuscript is entitled:

Bibliotheca Heberiana / Catalogue / of / the Library / of the / late / Richard Heber, Esq. / Part the eleventh. / Manuscripts.

Where and how Mr. Heber came into possession of the manuscript, and its exact history prior to his ownership, are unfortunately unknown. The excerpt from the Heber sale catalogue states:

1151–The Virginall Booke of Elizabeth Rogers, 1656, / containing Songs by Lawes, Brewer, & c. with the Names / of the

Tunes. It afterwards belonged to Sir T. Fairfax.

The reference to Sir Thomas Fairfax's ownership of the manuscript is currently unsupportable, although it has been suggested that the compiler of the catalogue may have had information which has since been lost. Thomas, Lord Fairfax did indeed have a large manuscript collection, which makes the conjecture not unfeasible, based as it also is on the idea that Sir Thomas would have been interested in a manuscript containing a setting entitled "Sir Thomas Fairfax's March" (f. 2).

The name "John Tillett" occurs once (f. 2) but nothing is known of him. *The Catalogue of Manuscript Music in the British Museum*, volume III, indicates that he may have been an owner during the eighteenth century. Some notations in a hand presumably his support this hypothesis on the basis of spellings and calligraphy.

Elizabeth Rogers, thus far, remains anonymous. The manuscript bears the inscription (f. 1b) "Elizabeth Rogers hir virginall booke. Ffebruary $\overset{e}{y}$ 27 1656." The significance of this date is unknown. It may be the date of completion, presentation or commemoration of birthday or anniversary. Thanks

Fig. 1. The front cover of the manuscript of *Elizabeth Rogers hir virginall booke*. (Courtesy Trustees of the British Museum)

to references and composers' names within the manuscript, certain pieces are identifiable as contemporary with the date of the manuscript; others are older. For example, the suite *The Battle* appears in *My Ladye Nevells Booke*, completed in 1591. "Essex's Last Goodnight" was a popular tune at least as early as 1576 and had a revived popularity in 1601.

On folio 1 is twice written the name "Elizabeth Fayre," whose initials are also stamped on the binding (see Figure 1). It has been suggested that these two Elizabeths are one person, before and after marriage, but at present this must remain only a suggestion.

PHYSICAL DESCRIPTION OF THE MANUSCRIPT

The manuscript is a bound folio volume of evidently prelined pages. The musical numbers 1 through 65, 77 through 80 and 84 through 94 are in their natural positions, while numbers 66 through 76, 81 through 83 and 95 through 112 appear inverted. This is because the manuscript had been turned back to front at some time and inverted to present a set of fresh pages for the beginning of the Vocal Lessons. These inverted pieces (excluding numbers 81, 82 and 83) were apparently added at a slightly later date.

The manuscript seems to be written in four different hands. The first (numbers 1 through 65 and 77 through 94) seems to be a carefully schooled hand and, except for certain calligraphic modifications as the work progresses, remains fairly uniform throughout. It is probably the hand of a scribe or music teacher. The second hand (numbers 66 through 76, 95 through 104 and 107 through 109) is a less formal one and, comparing it to the signature of Elizabeth Fayre (f. 1), may well be her own. The third (numbers 105 and 106) may well be that of the teacher of the Vocal Lessons, being as it is a neat, professional musical hand. A note concerning the tuning of the viol (see p. xxii below) is in the same writing, a fact which could lend much weight to the proposition that these pieces are in the hand of the teacher of the Vocal Lessons. The last hand (numbers 110 through 112) is neat as far as the lyrics are concerned but the music is unkempt.

Figures 2 through 4 reproduce three manuscript pages, identified in the captions.

As published here, the order of pieces 1 through 94 is exactly as it occurs in the manuscript, page by page, the inverted pages being righted. Pieces 95 through 112 are not only righted but also reversed from their natural order to comply with a partial table of contents of the Vocal Lessons in the manuscript (f. 60).

The verbal notations in the manuscript are of some interest in that they contain some poetic fragments and notes by various people and give also an insight into the personality of Elizabeth Rogers-Fayre, in whose hand most of them seem to be written. The front flyleaf (f. 1) contains an incomplete table of contents; twice the name "Elizabeth Fayre," once surrounded by scribbled ornament; some other scribbled ornaments; and the following poetic fragments:

Time and Tide / Stayes ffor none here
(Time and Tide stays for none here)

where loue by grace hath / possesone the parting kiss the / deap inpreson.
(Where love by grace hath possession, the parting kiss the deep impression.)
This Is The dart that pearst the hart the / Constant loue to try ffor Fame still / And euer will bee Constant tell I dy. / A hart I haue And that Is ffree my only / Joy I geue to the Iff thin bee soo and bee / not gone then lett us goyne our harts In one.
(This is the dart that pierced the heart, the constant love to try; for Fame still and ever will be constant till I die. A heart I have, and that is free. My only joy I give to thee. If thine be so and be not gone, then let us join our hearts in one.)

The other side of the flyleaf (f. 1b) contains an incomplete table of contents, including numbers 1 through 18, 20 through 65 and 77 through 94. It is a point of interest that this list indicates the manuscript originally had a leaf at the beginning containing on one side two pieces entitled "Preludium" and "An Almaine," and on the other side, "Philena" and "Corrante." This page was missing at the time of purchase by the British Museum and it is not known at what point it was lost. Drexel MS 5609 in the collection of the New York Public Library is a transcription of a number of early keyboard manuscripts, among which is the beginning portion of *Elizabeth Rogers hir virginall booke*. This transcription was apparently made in the mid-eighteenth century and these four pieces were missing at that time.

The rear flyleaf (f. 60) contains an incomplete table of contents for the Vocal Lessons (numbers 95 through 105 and 107 through 110) and the poetic fragment:

In Excese off ioy and payne / I doue labour to obtaine / Such A measure / off Loues Treasure /

Fig. 2.   Folio 42b, containing the complete music of number 87, ''Love
Is Strange.'' (Courtesy Trustees of the British Museum)

Fig. 3. Folio 33, containing the complete music of number 69, "The Spaniard," and number 70 (untitled). (Courtesy Trustees of the British Museum)

Fig. 4. Folio 54, containing the complete music, and the first verse of the lyric, of number 103, "O That Mine Eyes." (Courtesy Trustees of the British Museum)

That I bee not poure againe. // when I pyne
with staruing care / Hope does so enlarge my
ffeaires / As not ffearing willowe wareing /
More I loue the more I dayre.
(In excess of joy and pain, I do labor to obtain
such a measure of Love's treasure that I be not
poor again. When I pine with starving care,
Hope does so enlarge my fears, as not fearing,
willow wearing; more I love, the more I dare.

The other side of this leaf (f. 60b) bears the fragment:

Sith hart and break thou mast no longer liue /
Injoy this world nothing that I wold giue / I liue
forlorne all goyes are ffrom me ffleed / Iue lost
my loue Alase my hart is dead.
(Since, heart, and break thou must, no longer
live. To enjoy this world nothing that I would
give. I live forlorn; all joys are from me fled.
I've lost my love. Alas! My heart is dead.
(see no. 108, Analytical Notes.)

At the foot of folio 2 is the (accurate) notation,
apparently in the hand of John Tillett, that "The
names of most of these tunes are / at the end of
each." At certain places throughout the manuscript
this same hand has repeated the title of the piece at
the head of the page.

THE VIRGINAL

The virginal is a rectangular relative of the harpsichord. Its sound is produced, as in all members of
this family, by plectra plucking the strings. At the
rear of each key, held upright in a rack called a
register, is a small piece of wood (plastic or metal in
some modern instruments) called a jack. This jack
has inserted in it a pivoting, spring-loaded tongue
(wood, metal or plastic) which holds the plectrum
(traditionally quill or leather, plastic in most
modern instruments) perpendicular to the string.
When the front of the key is depressed, the back
rises, forcing the jack, and with it the plectrum,
upward, thereby causing the plectrum to pluck the
string, effecting a sound. When the key is released,
the jack drops back to its original place. The plectrum is enabled to fall back past the string without
replucking it because of the pivoting ability of the
tongue. A damper, attached to the upper part of the
jack, rests on the string, keeping it mute until it is
raised off the string by the upward movement of the
jack. When the jack falls back to its rest position, the
damper once more rests on the string and silences it.
The term "virginal" (often referred to in the

plural, "virginals" or "a pair of virginals") was
used as a generic term for all plucked keyboard
instruments until the middle of the seventeenth century, when it gradually came to refer specifically to
the rectangular member of the family. It must not be
thought, then, that the harpsichord or spinet are in
any way historically incorrect instruments for performance of the pieces of this collection.

The idea is often set forth that virginals were so
called because they were most often played upon by
maidens or virgins (the titles of the collections
Parthenia and *Parthenia In-Violata* contain puns on the
subject of maidenhood). The word is thought by
some, however, to have its true basis in the Latin
virgula, meaning a small bit of wood or a stick. This
would refer to the jacks and/or the keys and might
easily have been used in an age when Latin was the
language of intelligent communication. In this case,
however, one cannot discount the propensity, indeed
the mania, of the Englishmen of that time to incor-
porate a pun or double-entendre whenever the
opportunity permitted. If the term *was* derived from
Latin, it is fairly obvious that within a generation or
two the original source of the word was completely
overshadowed by its new, more popular meaning,
especially as Latin had begun to fall into disuse as the
vehicle for written communication.

SURVEY OF VIRGINAL MUSIC,
AND THE MUSIC OF THE PRESENT WORK

The advanced technique of virginal music which
developed in the latter part of the sixteenth century
seems to have had no foundation in previous keyboard
tradition. Composition for the organ, because of that
instrument's nature, was originally directly related to
the perfectly balanced counterpoint of polyphonic
vocal music. With the rise and growing importance
of secular music published or in manuscript, especially the advancement of popular song and dance
forms, perfectly organized counterpoint gave way to
a new sense of accented rhythm and, by association,
a new sense of vertical harmony, harmony as an entity
rather than as a function of melody. Compounding
these developments, the English school of lutenists
came to prominence and, because of the nature of the
lute and its empirical methods, added much impetus
to this evolution. The virginalists followed closely
and quickly in the steps of the lutenists, adding to the
innovations of the latter the idioms of the keyboard.
Earlier examples of virginal music, rudimentary
though they be, already demonstrate the variation

form, the melodic and rhythmic sequential writing and the involved scale passages that became so highly developed in the keyboard writing of the turn of the century.

Keyboard music was the last genre of music to be commercially reproduced because of the complex printing problems not encountered in music for other instruments. These obstacles made the venture too difficult and financially unfeasible. The first commercially reproduced edition, *PARTHENIA | or | THE MAYDENHEAD | of the first musicke that | ever was printed for the Virginalls*, appeared in 1612–13 and was not followed by another edition until 1624–25, when *PARTHENIA IN-VIOLATA. | or | THE MAYDEN-MUSICKE for the Virginalls and Bass-Viol* appeared. Both of these editions were ultimately engraved and not typeset as other music was. In an age in which the ability to perform music in some manner was considered a *sine qua non* of the complete lady or gentleman, and in which the virginals was the common household instrument, this cannot be considered a very prolific outpouring of keyboard music. It is for this reason that there are many manuscript keyboard collections extant. Most of these collections take the form of commonplace-books, that is, books of favorite pieces and lessons compiled for a certain person, whose name often appears inscribed in the manuscript. Among such collections are the virginal books of Benjamin Cosyn, Will Forster (manuscripts in the British Museum) and Lady Nevell, to name a few, and a large number of unnamed complete and fragmentary manuscripts.

The present manuscript is of special interest because of its very personal insight into the everyday music-making of the age. It is not so involved, technical and impersonal as the Fitzwilliam collection or *My Ladye Nevells Booke*, nor is it so vague as most of the unnamed fragmentary collections.* The pieces are not so simple that they should be overlooked, nor are they so complex that they are restricted to professional performance. This is, in a sense, music for the amateur performer, in the true sense of amateur, an accomplished and knowledgeable lover, the type with which the era was filled. These pieces were the sort that would graciously fill an evening in the entertainment of guests and friends. There are settings of popular tunes, some original works and some vocal pieces in which guests might participate by singing or taking up the viol. They were also suitable for the

display of a maiden's gentle accomplishments before an ardent suitor. Whatever their use, they are ideal examples of music-making at home in an age in which, as North (1653–1734) points out in *The Musical Grammarian*,† "many chose rather to fidle at home, then to goe out and be knockt on the head abroad."

The work is of musicological interest as an example of transitional writing from late Renaissance to early Baroque. Some of the pieces display such late Renaissance features as settings of popular tunes, variation style, some internal rhythmic changes, vestiges of early notation, uneven barring and modal writing. Side by side with these are also found tonàl writing, some uniform methods of notation, the beginnings of the traditional suite (based on the allemande-courant pair rather than the pavane-galliard pair of the earlier period) and the greater importance of the outermost voices — all characteristic of the later period. The vocal music is an example of the *stile recitativo* so popular at the time, the madrigal having declined in favor, probably through the influence of Italian opera.

With regard to the musical forms represented here:

"Almaine" was the common English usage for allemande. The allemande is a dance form in duple meter, of moderate tempo, of a more sweet than frivolous air. It traditionally is composed of two sections, each repeated, of which the second is usually longer. Ideally, the allemande should begin on an upbeat.

The courant is a dance form in triple meter (usually 3/2), moderately fast in tempo and joyous in spirit, with a characteristic predominance of dotted rhythms. It traditionally consists of two sections also, each repeated, and should begin ideally on an upbeat. As the courant became removed from the dance and developed more toward an abstract musical form, it underwent a rhythmic modification. In its early stages the courant was often found with its last measure counted in 6/4 rather than 3/2 time. Courants later came to be found with both rhythms used throughout the piece and eventually entirely in 6/4. These last two cases seem to apply to the courants in this collection.

The sarabande was originally a dance of such sensuous grace that its performance was considered punishable under the law. As the dance progressed into the courts and later grew to be a musical form, it lost the wanton nature of its portrayal, retaining only the grace, becoming a dance of great majesty and

---

* *The Fitzwilliam Virginal Book*, edited by J. A. Fuller Maitland and W. Barclay Squire, 1899 (Dover reprint, 1963); *My Ladye Nevells Booke*, edited by Hilda Andrews, 1926 (Dover reprint, 1969).

† Edited by Hilda Andrews, 1926.

grandeur. It is traditionally in triple meter with the accent falling on the second beat. It is written in two sections, and as in the allemande and courant, each section is repeated. The repetitions of the sarabande, however, are often played with a great deal of ornament and division.

These three dance forms, originally the allemande-courant pair and later the sarabande with it, became the foundation of the suite, which reached a perfection in the orchestral suites, partitas and French and English suites of Johann Sebastian Bach.

THE COMPOSERS REPRESENTED

All the keyboard pieces of this collection are included anonymously. Only a few of the vocal pieces have composers' names attached to them, and these names have been noted in the Analytical Notes in their original spellings. Other pieces have been attributed to certain composers by consultation of other sources.

The "Mr. Balles" of the manuscript may be Richard Balls, who was a wait (public musician) of the city of London for music and voice. He died probably in 1622, since application was made on 21 October of that year to replace him with a "John Willson," possibly the John Wilson of this collecttion (see below).

Thomas Brewer (1611–?) was enrolled at the age of three years as a student at Christ's Hospital, where he apparently studied the viol with the music-master of the school. Little is known of Brewer's life although he was well known as a viol player and his works were included in many printed collections. The following anecdote concerning Brewer is included in a manuscript collection by Sir Nicholas L'Estrange entitled *Merry Passages and Jeasts* (British Museum, Harl. 6395):

> Thom: Brewer, my Mus: seruant, through his Pronenesse to good-Fellowshippe, hauing attaind to a very Rich and Rubicund Nose; being reproued by a Friend for his too frequent vse of strong Drinkes and Sacke; as very Pernicious to that Distemper and Inflamation in his Nose. Nay — Faith, sayes he, if it will not endure sack, it's no Nose for me.

William Byrd (ca. 1540–1623), who is not mentioned directly in the manuscript but who is known to be the composer of the *Battle* suite, needs little introduction as one of the foremost keyboard and vocal composers of Elizabethan England. On 22 February 1569, he was sworn as a gentleman of the Chapel Royal. He was a student of Thomas Tallis and

with him served as an organist of the Chapel Royal. On 22 January 1575, Tallis and Byrd were granted exclusive right by Elizabeth I to print and sell music, domestic and foreign, and music paper for the period of twenty-one years. It is interesting to note that Byrd, as were many of the Gentlemen of the Chapel Royal, was a known Catholic partisan even though he outwardly conformed to the state religion. For most of his life he lived outside London, which may have served to keep his (and more so his wife's) religious beliefs out of the center of attention — although he and his family were brought before the religious court of Essex for "popish" practices and were later known as "papisticall recusants." All these things considered, he was nevertheless regularly called upon at court by both Elizabeth I and James I, who were apparently willing to overlook the religious problem for brilliant hands at the keyboard or a pleasing new tune.

Orlando Gibbons (1583–1625), also not specifically mentioned in the manuscript, was for most of his youth a chorister in the choir of King's College, Cambridge. On 21 March 1604, he was appointed organist of the Chapel Royal. His works were first published in *Parthenia* in 1611–12 with those of William Byrd and John Bull. Gibbons seems to have been steadily at work until he died of a kind of apoplectic seizure. He was apparently a regular in the household of Sir Christopher Hatton, who is credited by Gibbons with the composition of the lyrics of his first published madrigals. His pieces for viols are among the first written idiomatically for the instrument; earlier the instrument merely took over a vocal part.

Robert Johnson was a member of Sir Thomas Kytson's household as early as 1574. He came to London not later than 1610, when he is described as a musician to Shakespeare's company and second in ability on the lute only to John Dowland. In 1611 he was a musician to Henry, Prince of Wales, upon whose death he became a musician to Prince Charles, later Charles I. He composed much music for plays, including Shakespeare's *The Tempest*, Beaumont and Fletcher's *Valentinian* and Ben Jonson's *Masque of the Gypsies*. The dates of his birth and death are still unknown.

Henry Lawes (1596–1662) was a student of Giovanni Coperario and brother of William Lawes (see below). On 1 January 1626, he was sworn as epistler of the Chapel Royal and on 3 November of the same year became a gentleman of the Chapel Royal. In 1631 he was appointed "musician in ordinary for the lutes and voices'' in the King's Musick. He was praised for his settings, in which he made the prosody of the text the foremost consideration. For this reason the best poets of the day, including Waller and Milton, desired that their works be set to music by him. This was the beginning of the vocal style which reached a peak in the songs of Henry Purcell. Lawes was the teacher of the children of the Earl of Bridgewater — Lord Brackley, Mr. Thomas Egerton and Lady Alice Egerton — who all took part in (and were in fact the inspiration for) the masque *Comus*, with text by Milton and music by Lawes, first presented on Michaelmas night, 1634, at Ludlow Castle. Lawes took part in this performance as well. Upon the dissolution of the court at the outbreak of the civil wars, Henry Lawes took to teaching music to the children of other wealthy and noble families. To judge by the choice of composers and music in the Vocal Lessons, it would not be impossible, although unlikely to be proven at present, that Lawes was the music teacher, for voice and viol, of Elizabeth Rogers, or Fayre. At Trinity College, Cambridge, there are three manuscript copies of the following sonnet to Henry Lawes by John Milton (the first, a rough draft in Milton's hand, is headed ''To my friend Mr. Hen. Laws Feb. 9. 1645''; the other two, one in Milton's hand and the other in that of an amanuensis, are headed ''To Mr Hen. Laws on his Aires''):

> Harry whose tuneful and well measur'd Song
> First taught our English Musick how to span
> Words with just note and accent, not to scan
> With Midas Ears, committing short and long;
> Thy worth and skill exempts thee from the throng,
> With praise anough [*sic*] for Envy to look wan;
> To after-age thou shalt be writ the man,
> That with smooth aire couldst humor best our
>   tongue.
> Thou honour'st Verse, and Verse must lend her
>   wing
> To honour thee, the Priest of Phoebus Quire
> That tun'st their happiest lines in Hymn, or Story.
> Dante shall give Fame leave to set thee higher
> Then his Casella, whom he woo'd to sing,
> Met in the milder shades of Purgatory.

William Lawes (1602–1645), brother of Henry Lawes, received his early musical training under Coperario, the Earl of Hertford paying the cost. This may be taken as an indication of his talent in music. William Lawes seems to have been very popular at court even before he was sworn a gentleman of the Chapel Royal on 30 April 1635. During his time at court, both before and after his appointment, he composed a great deal of music for masques and set many Psalm verses to music although none of his works were published until after his death. Thomas Fuller, in *The History of the Worthies of England* (1662), relates the circumstances of Lawes' death during his term of duty in the Royalist army during the civil wars:

> In these distracted times his Loyalty ingaged him in the War for his Lord and Master and though he was by General Gerrard made a Commissary on designe to secure him (such Officers being commonly shot-free by their place, as not Exposed to danger) yet such the activity of his Spirit, he disclaimed the Covert of his Office, and betrayed thereunto by his own adventurousness was casually shot at the Siege of Chester, the same time when the Lord Bernard Stuart lost his life.
>
> Nor was the Kings soul so ingrossed with grief for the death of so near a Kinsman, and Noble a Lord Bernard Stuart, but that hearing of the death of his deare seruant William Lawes, he had a particular Mourning for him when dead, whom he loved when living, and commonly called the Father of Musick.

The following lines, probably by one Thomas Jordan, were written upon the death of William Lawes:

> On Mr. William Lawes, Musician, slain at the
>   siege of West Chester.
>
> Concord is conquer'd; in this urn there lies
> The Master of great Music's Mysteries;
> And in it is a riddle like the cause,
> Will. Lawes was slain by those whose Wills were
>   Laws.

Nicholas Laniere (1588–1666), not specifically mentioned in the manuscript, was, like many other members of his family, a musician in the royal household. He was attached to the household of Henry, Prince of Wales, until the death of the prince in 1612. For the next few years he remained at court, composing much music for masques. In 1625, at the accession of Charles I, Laniere was appointed master of the King's music. Being a painter as well as musician, he was sent by the King in 1625 to collect works of art on the Continent for the royal collection. At the outbreak of the civil wars, Laniere's fortunes declined and during the period of the Commonwealth and the Protectorate he appears to have accompanied the royal family into exile in the Low Countries. At the Restoration he was reinstated as master of the King's music and remained in service until his death.

John Wilson (1595–1674) was a lutenist, violist, singer and composer. He became one of the King's musicians in 1635. He was favored at court and at Oxford, the major center of musical activity. He was considered "the best at the lute in all England," a title held previously by John Dowland and Robert Johnson. At the famous music meetings at Oxford, he often played his lute for the company and usually presided over the consort. It is also reported that while he was in the service of the King (Charles I) he "frequently played to him, when the king would usually lean on his shoulder." In 1646 he became a member of the household of Sir William Walter, the court having been dissolved because of the wars. In 1656, when the professorship of music was reestablished at Oxford, Wilson was appointed. In 1661 he resigned that post to become a chamber musician to Charles II, and in 1662 replaced the deceased Henry Lawes as a gentleman of the Chapel Royal. There is some discussion as to whether or not this John Wilson is the same as the John (or Jack) Wilson who seems to have been involved with the theaters of London in the first part of the century. In 1622 there is a letter soliciting for a "John Willson" the place of one of the waits of the city, which was made vacant by the death of Richard Balls (see above). The 1623 folio of Shakespeare's *Much Ado About Nothing* (Act ii, Scene 3) gives the stage direction, "Enter the Prince, Leonato, Claudio, and Jacke Willson." This indicates that "Jacke Willson" would have taken the part of Balthazar and sung "Sigh No More, Ladies." We know that the lutenist John Wilson had much to do with composers who did set music for the stage; and we know that a "Mr. Willson yᵉ singer" was among the guests at the anniversary of the famous actor Edward Alleyn, and that an autograph inscription in a copy of Ben Jonson's collected *Workes* reads: "To his most worthy and learned friend, Mr. John Wilson, Ben Jonson's Guift and testimony of his love." Wilson is also known to have been responsible for at least some of the music of *The Maske of Flowers*, presented by the gentlemen of Gray's Inn on Twelfth Night, 1614. Also Wilson, in his later publications, printed several songs from plays, including Shakespeare's "Take O Take Those Lips Away" and "Lawn as White as Driven Snow." Wilson was reputed to have been "a great Humourist and pretender to Buffoonry," and Sir Nicholas L'Estrange reports in his manuscript, *Merry Passages and Jeasts*:

> Willson, and Har: and Will: Lawes were at a Taverne one night; Wilson being in worst case of the three, swore he would Quarrell with the

next Man he mett, who was a meere stranger and a sober gentleman; whome he thus accosted; are you not a Catholicke? yes marry am I; Then ya're a Knave says he; the Gentl: having past by a little way, stepps backe to him; and bids him not swallow an Error, for sayes he, I am no Catholicke: why then ya're a scurvy Lying Knave sayes Willson. Upon that out flew their swords, but the Lawes parted them presently.

As a postscript to the list of composers, Thomas Strengthfield, who has been taken to be the composer of a number of pieces of the collection, may well have been the virginal teacher of Elizabeth Rogers. Unfortunately, nothing can be found concerning him, so this must remain entirely hypothetical.

POLITICAL HISTORY OF THE AGE

The date of the manuscript, 1656, falls during the Protectorate of Oliver Cromwell, implying that the pieces for the most part precede that date although some of the Vocal Lessons may well have been written after the Restoration. Since the earliest pieces are dated from the reign of Elizabeth I, a brief historical outline follows, beginning with her reign and ending with the Restoration of Charles II.

Elizabeth ascended the throne in 1558 and ruled England through one of its most glorious eras, when it rose to a pinnacle of artistic prominence. Politically, however, it was a period of uncertainty and controversy generated by religious changes initiated by Elizabeth's father, Henry VIII, when he separated England from the Church of Rome. Steering a middle course between Roman Catholicism on the one hand and the more extreme Protestant sects on the other, Elizabeth established the Church of England, with England's sovereign as the Church's "supreme governor." Throughout her reign she had to defend her Church from the assaults of both the Catholics and the extreme Protestant sects who, because of their efforts to "purify" the Church of England and cleanse it of Catholic doctrines, came to be known as "Puritans."

At Elizabeth's death in 1603, James VI of Scotland succeeded to England's throne as James I. He was a strong believer in absolute monarchy and spent much of his reign in conflict with Parliament, which was falling under the control of the Puritans. Henry, Prince of Wales, James's oldest son, died in 1612 so that when James died in 1625, he was succeeded on the throne by his second son, Charles I.

Although Charles I was a personable individual with a keen appreciation for the arts, he inherited his father's political and religious inflexibility. He resisted Parliament's repeated attempts to ''purify'' the Church of England and infuriated the Puritans by marrying the devoutly Catholic daughter of the King of France. When Parliament retaliated by refusing to vote adequate moneys and supplies to support the King's government, Charles decided to rule as an absolute monarch without Parliament. During this period of personal rule, 1629 to 1640, Charles was forced to raise money by dubious means. When he attempted to impose the Church of England on staunchly Presbyterian Scotland, the Scots rebelled and invaded England. In order to bring the Scots to heel, Charles was forced to recall Parliament. The Parliament which he called in 1640 was dominated by the Puritans and was determined to curb the powers of the king. This conflict led to the outbreak of the Civil War between Parliament (called Puritans or Round-heads) and the Royalists (or Cavaliers). The Parliamentary army under the leadership of Sir Thomas Fairfax and Oliver Cromwell eventually defeated and captured Charles. The army then took control of Parliament and brought the king to trial for treason. On 30 January 1649, Charles was executed and England, for the first and only time in its history, was without a monarch.

In 1649 Parliament declared England a Common-wealth, but the ineptitude of the new government led Oliver Cromwell in 1653 to establish a new system of government with himself at its head as ''Lord Protector.'' For the next five years, Cromwell ruled virtually as a monarch until his death in 1658, when he was succeeded by his son, Richard Cromwell (shades of the old monarchy). Richard was a man without political ambitions who retired at the earliest opportunity. The ensuing military power struggle ended when General George Monck took control of London, recalled Parliament and decided to restore the monarchy. Charles, son of the executed Charles I, had been living in exile in the Netherlands and was now invited to return to his kingdom. On 25 May 1660, Charles II landed at Dover and four days later, amid joyous celebrations, entered London as the King Restored.

The music in the present volume is a startling commentary on these historic events. The *Battle* suite, the marches of Sir Thomas Fairfax (the Parliamentary general) and of Prince Rupert (the Royalist general), ''Rupert's Retreat,'' the ''Scots March,''

the songs of the Protectorate in ''The King's Complaint'' and of the hoped-for Restoration in ''When the King Enjoys His Own Again'' and ''What if the King Should Come to the City'' — all these seem to be a vital portrayal of the feelings of an era reflected in art. Elizabeth Rogers, or perhaps more realistically her family, seems to have had Royalist affiliations and this political atmosphere has crept in and settled in the instrumental pages of her music book. The vocal music then returns to the gentle masquing airs and heartsick songs of the courtly life and the strife is forgotten. The remainder of the pieces are the pastoral pastimes of a gentle life.

PRINCIPLES OF THE PRESENT EDITION AND TRANSCRIPTION

The editorial methods employed in the present transcription are an attempt to convey as much of the character and form of the pieces of the original manuscript as is possible, at the same time using techniques of notation readily accessible to the modern performer without the addition of editorial symbols.

In the manuscript, numbers 1 through 95 are written on staves of six lines each. Numbers 96 through 112 are written on staves of five lines. In the transcription, these have all been standardized to the modern system of five-line staves.

Moveable *G*, *F* and *C* clefs are used in the manuscript, the latter one often in conjunction with the former two. The moveable clefs were often employed for little reason other than to avoid the use of leger lines. The transcription has been standardized to second-line *G* clef for the treble and fourth-line *F* clef for the bass according to the usual modern system. The calligraphic forms of the clefs in the transcription closely resemble those of the manuscript and are closely related to the letter symbols which they indicate.

The time signatures used in the manuscript are remnants of the Medieval-Renaissance system of the Greater and Lesser Prolation. The symbols were originally employed to indicate the division of the larger note values into two or three beats. With the advent of accented rhythm came barlines, which adequately indicated this division regardless of their irregularity in early music. Only two symbols of this system survive in the manuscript, ₵ (usually accompanied and sometimes replaced by the numerals three or three-one, indicating the presence of the old ''tripla'') and ₵ . While these signs had a more specific significance in earlier unbarred music, in this case they indicate triple and duple time, respectively. These symbols have been maintained in the transcription, both at the beginnings of pieces and at internal rhythmic changes, even though in the latter situation they are for the most part superfluous for the following reason. In the case of "tripla" occurring throughout a piece, the subdivided minim has been altered to a dotted minim and the entire piece transcribed in triple time. When tripla occur incidentally with duple time in any piece, the minim has been maintained unaltered and the tripla have been transcribed as triplet crotchets. In these instances, it was considered more accessible to employ the modern triplet than to change the unit minim to a dotted minim, or vice versa, which might give the mistaken impression of lengthening or shortening a measure. For this reason the rhythmic symbols within the manuscript become unnecessary even though they remain indicative. Related to this is the fact that the original, frequently irregular, barlines have been retained from the manuscript, thereby often making modern numerical time signatures unsuitable. Double barlines are from the manuscript in all cases. The final double barlines have been added according to the modern system of a thick and a thin line. Any markings after such a barline are entirely ornamental, after the style of the original.

The notation of the manuscript has been entirely transcribed according to the modern system to render it more accessible to the modern performer. In certain situations, specifically in the vocal music, irregular groups of notes (e.g. rhythmic groups of five or seven notes to the beat) have been joined under the modern markings $\overbrace{5}$, $\overbrace{7}$ et cetera. Most of these exceptions are in the nature of ornaments. Quavers and their subdivisions have been uniformly grouped according to the modern practice of barred flags except when the grouping in the manuscript is obviously an indication of phrasing. The vocal music has been annotated according to the traditional syllabic system with regard to these specific note types. Rests have been included just as they occur in the manuscript. No attempt has been made to complete voices within a measure with appropriate rests, especially since the voice leading in these cases is usually obvious.

Key signatures are exactly as they occur in the manuscript. Any that are obviously lacking are corrected by the insertion of accidentals within the piece rather than at the beginning. Any accidental occurring in the manuscript also occurs in the transcription, appearing directly *before* the note to which it applies.

Sharps which are employed to naturalize a previously flatted note and flats which are employed to naturalize a previously sharped note, that is, accidentals which serve the function of the modern natural sign, have been transcribed as naturals to avoid confusion even though the symbol was not yet in use at the time. Any editorial accidental appears directly *above* or *below* the note to which it applies. These editorial additions are almost invariably in the nature of *musica ficta*. They are added in cases in which melody and harmony are rendered more concordant according to traditional rules. Since the modern convention that any accidental remains in effect until the subsequent barline or until it is cancelled by another accidental was then nonexistent, the inclusion of accidentals in the manuscript is often irregular, sometimes affecting the whole measure, sometimes only the note to which it applies. Editorial accidentals apply only to specific notes. Other than in the case of accidentals, when occasion has warranted the changing the pitch of a note or a group of notes (to correct errors by the copyist or to improve obviously faulty voice leading or harmony), the changes occur in the transcription with a parenthetical numerical notation referring to the Analytical Notes at the end of the volume, wherein the original pitches are recorded. These few changes will explain themselves if the piece is played in its original unaltered form.

Regarding repetition signs, any that appear in the manuscript have been retained in their original positions; no new ones have been added. When the manuscript implies (usually by cipher indications) that a repetition should occur but this is not marked with appropriate signs, the symbol 𝄋 and the words *dal segno* have been inserted in the appropriate positions to delineate the repetition. When the manuscript implies (by the same indications) that a repetition should be from the beginning of the piece, *da capo* has been inserted. In certain instances there is a small numeral "2" over a double barline, which has been taken to indicate a repetition; these have also been retained. As a note on performance, it may be said that any section marked off by double barlines may be repeated, often very effectively with divisions and ornaments. It may also be noted that measures containing repetition signs have been transcribed exactly as they exist in the manuscript, often containing both the repetition and the continuation in the same measure, sometimes giving it the impression of being unrhythmic. This practice of not altering or rearranging these measures into first and second endings is in keeping with the thought that repetitions, and in fact the whole structure of the performance of a piece, are at the discretion of the performer and are not defined as a necessity, which the latter system might tend to indicate.

The ornamental symbols ♯ and ♪ are common in this and most other keyboard manuscripts and none have been added or deleted. There is some discussion regarding their execution.

The first and by far more common of the two, ♯, is usually executed as a mordent, inverted mordent, turn or trill. There is apparently no hard and fast rule. The inflection of the melody and the function and duration of the affected note have, of course, great influence on the choice of ornament. This symbol does not, however, necessarily indicate an ornament. It implies more an accent; and while this is possibly achieved on the virginal by one of the above-mentioned ornaments, it must not be forgotten that slurs, staccati et cetera are also effective means of accent. Let it be said then that this symbol implies accent, achieved at the discretion of the performer.

The other symbol, ♪, while it may also obviously serve as an indiscriminate accent, is generally considered to be correctly executed as an upward run of a third, the speed of which is also influenced by the note affected. Again, this choice is at the discretion of the performer. Some of the ornaments may even be effectively disregarded, if desired.

Another marking in the nature of an ornament is that which indicates the arpeggiation of chords. While it is generally accepted that any chord may be arpeggiated for its effect, there seems to be in this manuscript (in a very few instances) the mark ♭, which implies an arpeggiated chord. These have been retained in the transcription.

The vocal music of the collection occurs in two types of arrangements. One is as a completely harmonized piece with the melody as the uppermost voice. These pieces have been transcribed from two-stave systems, with the solo and accompanimental parts combined, to three-stave systems, on which the solo voice has been isolated from the accompaniment. The accompaniment of these pieces may also be effectively played as solo keyboard works. The annotated vocal ornaments have been transcribed on the solo staff as they appear in the manuscript, but have not been transcribed in the accompaniment. They have in that case been reduced to a single melodic note, parenthetically enclosed to indicate that such reductions are arbitrary and editorial. The other type of vocal arrangement con-

tains only the melody and a bass part on two-stave systems, which have been retained in their original state. The performance of these is indicated as being that of a solo voice accompanied by a bass instrument or a basso continuo, that is, by a bass instrument playing the bass line and a harmonic instrument filling in harmonies. The bass line, as was often the case at the time, bears little or no indication of the harmonic realization, as it did at a later time, except in the setting of "Fire! Fire!" in which figures indicating suspensions and major thirds above the bass occur in a few instances. These figures, where they occur, have been moved from their position above the affected note to directly below the note to conform with the later practice and have been enclosed in brackets to eliminate confusion with editorial accidentals. These figures support the idea of harmonic realization in these pieces, and the use of a bass instrument, specifically the viol, in the manner of continuo is indicated by a notation regarding the tuning of the viol (f. 58b): "for the Tuning of the viole. / By notes / By Tablature or Letters." The retention of the original unrealized versions of these songs leaves to the performer or student the realization of these pieces at his own level of accomplishment, as would have been the case in the seventeenth century.

There are in the Vocal Lessons four vocal ornaments. Their apparent or traditional execution is as follows. The first, symbolized by ➚, indicates a slide or appoggiatura upwards from below; the next, ➘, indicates a slide or appoggiatura downwards from above; the next, ✗, is uncertain but may have been added at a later time and may indicate a trill of some sort; the final symbol, ⋰, also is uncertain but may indicate a rising and falling ornament or a repeated interruption of breath while singing a pitch. It is possible that all of these ornaments were added to the manuscript at a later date.

Regarding the literary transcriptions, certain basic rules have been followed. Form and syntax have been left unaltered. The spellings within the body of the transcription have all been modernized to render them more accessible and, especially in the case of lyrics, to lend ease in performance. The original spelling of both the titles and lyrics have been included with the Analytical Notes for scholarly interest. In certain instances, syllables have been moved ahead or behind a note if a word or phrase was rendered more singable by doing so.

Elizabeth Rogers

Hir Virginall Booke

1. Sir Thomas Fairfax's March

da capo

1

2. Nan's Masque

3. Almaine

4. The Fairest Nymphs the Valleys or Mountains Ever Bred

5. The Scots March

da capo

4

6. Prince Rupert's March

7. One of the Symphonies

8. One of the Symphonies

9. Sarabande

10. When the King Enjoys His Own Again

8

11. Almaine

12. A Trumpet Tune

13. Essex's Last Goodnight

14. Almaine by Thomas Strengthfield

15. The Courant to the Last Almaine by Thomas Strengthfield

16. Rupert's Retreat

17. Almaine by Thomas Strengthfield

18. Courant to the Former Almaine by Thomas Strengthfield

19.

20. The Nightingale

21. Courant Beare

22. Sarabande Beare

dal segno

23. Courant Beare

dal segno

24. Almaine

da capo

25. Courant

dal segno

26. Courant Beare—

27. Courant Beare

The Battle
Nos 28 through 39

28. The Soldiers' Summons

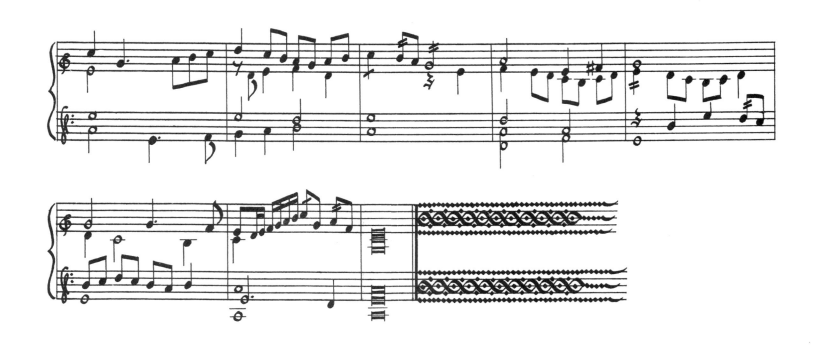

29. The March of Foot

30. The March of Horse

31. The Trumpets

32. The Irish March

33. Bagpipes

31

34. The Drum and Flute

35. The March to the Fight

36. Tarra-tantarra

37. The Battle Joined

38. Retreat

39. The Burying of the Dead

The End of the Battle

40. The Soldiers' Delight

41. Courant

42. Sarabande

43. A Masque

44. Courant

45. Sarabande

46. Lie Still, My Dear

Lie still, my dear. Why do'st thou rise? The light that

shines comes from thine eyes. The day breaks not, it

is my heart, to think that thou and I must part. Oh

Stay, Oh stay, Oh stay or else my joys must

die, and pe-rish in their in - fan-cy.

47. The Chestnut

48. Cloris Sighed

Clor-is sighed and sang and wept; sigh-ing sang, and sing - ing slept; and wakes; sighs, sings, and weeps a - gain for A-min - tas, Oh A-min - tas that was slain: Oh, Oh

49. Now ye Spring Is Come—

50. Oh Jesu Meek

Oh Je - su meek, Oh Je - su sweet; Oh Je - su Sav - iour mine: Most gra-cious Je - su to my call thy gra-cious ears in - cline.

51. Courant

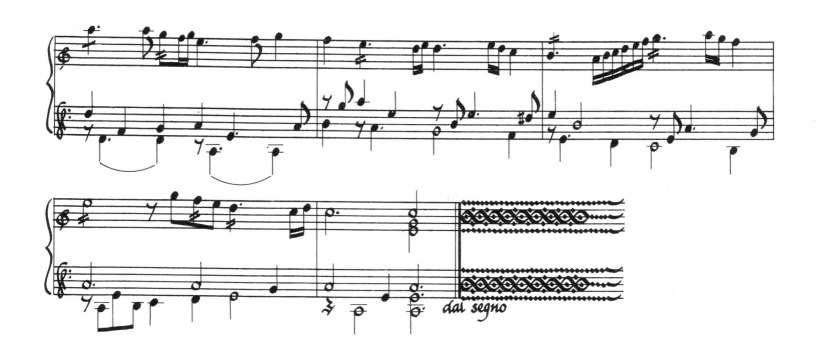

52. Courant

53. Masque

54. Courant

dal segno

55. Almaine

54

56. Lupus' Air

57. Could Thine Incomparable Eye—

Could thine in-com-par-a-ble eye beam forth, beam
forth, beam forth such am-a-bil-i-ty; then
has my win-ning pen the art my win-ning pen the art to steer,
to steer af-fec — tion and to charm your heart.

dal segno

dal segno

56

58. Almaine : Mr. Johnson

59. Mock-nightingale

60. What if the King Should Come to the City

61. The King's Complaint

62. Almaine

63. Courant

64. Sarabande

65. My Delight

66. A Scots Tune

67. An Irish Toy

68. Almaine

69. The Spaniard

70.

71. A Sarabande

72. The Phœnix

73. The Faithfull Brothers

14. A Courant

15. This Soldier Loves

Voice I

This sold-ier loves and fain would die to win. Shall he go

Voice II

in? No, 'tis too foul a sin, he must not come a-board.

I dare not row; storms of dis-pair and guilt-y blood will

Voice I   Voice II

blow. Shall time re-lease him say? O no, O no nor

time nor death can al-ter us nor prayers, My boat is Dest-i-

ny and who then dares but those ap-point-ed come a-board,

live still and love by rea-son mor-tal, not by will.

Voice I

And when thy night shall close up thine eyes, *Chorus* then come a-board

and pass; 'til then be wise, 'til then be wise.

76. Charon, O Charon

Voice I

Char-on, O Char-on, thou waft-er of the souls to bliss or bane.

Voice II

Who calls the ferr-y-man of Hell? *Voice I* Come near and say who lives in

joy and who in fear. Those that die well, e-tern-al joys shall

foll-ow; those that die ill, their own foul fate shall foll-ow.

Shall thy black bark those guilt-y spir-its stow that kill them-selves for

love? O no! O no! My cord-age creaks when such foul sins are

near. No wind blows fair, nor I my-self can steer. What spir-its pass and

in El-y-sium reign? Those gen-tle souls that are be-loved a-gain

77. Hornpipe

78. Almaine

79. Courant by Thomas Strengthfield

80. Sarabande

81. Almaine

82. Courant

83. Almaine

84. I wish no more

I wish no more thou should'st love me. My joys are full in lov - ing thee. My heart's too nar-row to con - tain my bliss if thou should'st love a - gain.

85.

86. *Sarabande: Thomas Strengthfield*

87. Love Is Strange

88. Almaine Mercury

89. Glory of the North

90. Almaine

91. Mercury

92. Courant

93. Courant

94. Phil Porter's Lamentation

Vocal Lessons
Nos 95 through 112

95. Psalm 42

Lord, as the hart, em-bossed with heat, brays af-ter the cool riv-u-let; so sighs my soul for thee. My soul thirsts for the liv-ing god. When shall I en-ter his a-bode and there his beau - ty see?

96. Must Your Fair Inflaming Eye—

Must your fair in-flam-ing eye make a world in love as I; all con-sent-ing, no re-pent-ing; as you will to live or die.

2. Your fair looks and rare deserts
   Keep in awe my yielding heart;
   Yet by praying and obeying,
   I do hope to bear a part.

3. Yet though I should plainly see,
   Your disdain would murder me;
   'T would not fright me, but delight me
   That I might your martyr be.

97. Since 'Tis My Fate

Since 'tis my fate to be thy slave,

un - der such pi - ty thou would'st crave.
(1)   (2)   #

If 't were my for - tune so to be

to him that courts his dest - i - ny.
[#](3)

95

98. No Flatt'ring Pillow

No flatt'-ring pil-low, down — y bed;
up - on ye fat-al moss and wil-low,
I lay my much tor-ment-ed head; and
sigh and weep un-til I keep just pa — ces
with my sor-row. Thus hard-ly can so sad a man dist-
in-guish night from mor-row.

My day is clouded and my nights
In misty discontentment shrouded,
And left quiet loss to all delight.
Save but my crime,
I hold with time
No reck'ning book nor tally;
The fountains keep the tears I weep,
My grave lies in the valley.

99. Baloo, My Boy

Ba - loo, my boy; lie still and sleep. It
grieves me sore to see thee weep. Would'st thou be
quiet, I'd'st be as glad. Thy mourn-ing makes
my sor-row sad. Lie still, my boy. thy
moth-er's joy, thy fath-er could me great an -
noy. La-loo, ba-loo, la-loo, la-loo, la-loo, la-loo, la-

loo,   ba-loo, ba-loo, ba-loo, ba-loo,   ba-loo,   ba-loo.

2. When he began to court my love—
   And with his sugared words did move,
   His flatt'ring face and feigned cheer
   To me that time did not appear.
   But now I see, that cruel he
   Cares neither for my boy, nor me.
   Baloo, baloo .....

3. But thou, my darling, sleep awhile,
   And when thou wakest, sweetly smile;
   Yet smile not as thy father did,
   To cozen maids; nay God forbid!
   But yet I fear that thou wilt here
   Thy father's face and heart still bear.
   Baloo, baloo .....

4. Now by my griefs I vow and swear
   Thee and all others to forbear.
   I'll never kiss nor cull nor clap,
   But tull my youngling in my lap.
   Cease, heart, to moan, leave off to groan
   And sleep securely, heart, alone.
   Baloo, baloo .....

100. I'll Wish No More

I'll wish no more thou should'st love me. My joys are full in lov-ing thee. My heart's too nar-row to con-tain my bliss if thou should'st love a-gain.

2. Thy scorns may wound me, but my fate
Leads me to love and thee to hate.
Yet must I love whilst I have breath,
For not to love were worse than death.

3. Then shall I sue for scorn or grace,
A ling'ring life or death embrace.
Since one of these I needs must try,
Love me but once and let me die.

101. Dearest Love, I Do Not Go

Dear-est love, I do not go, for
wear-i-ness of thee; or that all the
world can show a fit-ter love for me.
But since that I must die at last,
'tis best to use my-self in jest thus
by feign-ed death to die.

102. No, No! I Tell Ye No

No, no! I tell ye no! Though from thee I must go; yet my heart says not so. It swears by Stell-a's eyes, by whose dall-ying sur-prise it in Love's fet-ters lies. It swears by those ro-ses and lil-ies so white and those ru-bies so bright, ne'er to part, ne'er to part from my dear, dear de-light.

2. It swears by that warm snow in thy bosom below
   Where blind love hides his bow,
   And by those milk-white hands that dispense Cupid's bands
   And the quiver commands
   And let that form divine, and those small nimble feet,
   In love were too, too fleet,
   Ne'er to part, ne'er to part, Stella bright, Stella sweet.

3. By our true love it swears, by our hopes, by our fears,
   By our sad parting tears;
   And by this melting kiss, full of grief, full of bliss,
   By this too, and by this,
   And by this last embrace and this cruel adieu,
   And by high heaven, too,
   Ne'er to change, ne'er to change Stella's love for a new.

103. O That Mine Eyes

O that mine eyes could melt in-to a flood that I might plunge in tears for thee; as thou did'st swim in blood to ran - som me. O that this flesh-ly 'lem-bic would be - gin to drop, and drop a tear for ev' - ry sin.

2. See how his blood-bedabbled arms are spread
   To entertain death's welcome bands.
   Behold his bowing head,
   His bleeding hands,
   His oft-repeated stripes, his wounded side.
   Hark how he groaned; remember how he died.

3. The very heavens put weeds of sable on;
   The very rocks asunder rent;
   And yet this heart, that stone,
   Will not relent.
   Hard-hearted Man, for only Man denied
   To mourn for him, for whom he only died.

104. Yes, I Could Love

Yes, I could love, could I but find a mis-tress fit-ting to my mind. Whom nei-ther pride nor gold could move, to buy her beau-ty, sell her love; were neat, yet cared not to be fine and love me for my-self, not mine. not la-dy proud nor 'quett-ey coy but full of free-dom, full of joy.

Not wise enough to rule a state,
Nor fool enough to be laughed at;
Not childish young nor beldame old;
Not fiery hot nor icy cold;
Not richly proud nor basely poor;
Not chaste, yet no reputed whore:
If such a one I chance to find,
I have a mistress to my mind.

105. Let God, the God of Battle, Rise

Let god, the god of ba - ttle, rise and sca - tter his proud e - ne - mies. O, let them flee be - fore his face like smoke which dri - ving tem - pests chase; as wax di - ssolves with scor - ching fire, so pe - rish in his bur - ning ire.

106. Sing to the King of Kings

Sing to the King of kings; sing in un-u-sual lays; that hath wrought won-d'rous things, His con-quest crowned with praise, whose arm a-lone and sa-cred hands their im-pious bands have o-ver-thrown, their im-pious bands have o-ver-thrown.

107. Psalm 39, Verse 12

When Man for sin thy judge-ment feels,
just as a moth con-sumes a cloth, his beau-ty
fades, in strength he reels.
Man is all van-i-ty all van-i-ty and full of
ills. O spare me, Lord, O spare me, Lord
a while that I may gain some strength,

that I may gain some strength be-fore I die.

But, Lord, unto my prayers draw near;
Lend gracious ears
And see my tears;
On earth I am a sojourner
As all my fathers were.
O spare me, Lord.....

108. I Prithee, Sweet

I pri-thee, sweet, to me be kind; de-light not so in scor-ning.

I sue for love; O, let me find some plea-sure 'midst my mourn-ing.

What though to you I va-ssal be, let me my

right in-he-rit; send back the heart I gave to

thee since thine it can not me-rit. So I shall to the world de - clare

how wild, how naught and false you are.

109. Fire! Fire!

Fire! Fire! Lo! here I burn in such de-sire that all ye tears that I can strain out of mine emp-ty love-sick brain can not a-llay my scor-ching pain. Come, Hum-ber, Trent and sil-ver Thames; dread o-cean, haste with all thy streams; and if you can not quench my fire, O drown both me and my de-sire.

Fire! Fire!
There is no Hell to my desire.
See all the rivers backward fly
And the ocean doth his aid deny
For fear my heat should drink them dry.
Come, heavenly showers then, pouring down!
Come you that once the world did drown!
Some then you spared, but now save all
That else might burn and with me fall.

110. Come, You Pretty False-eyed Wanton

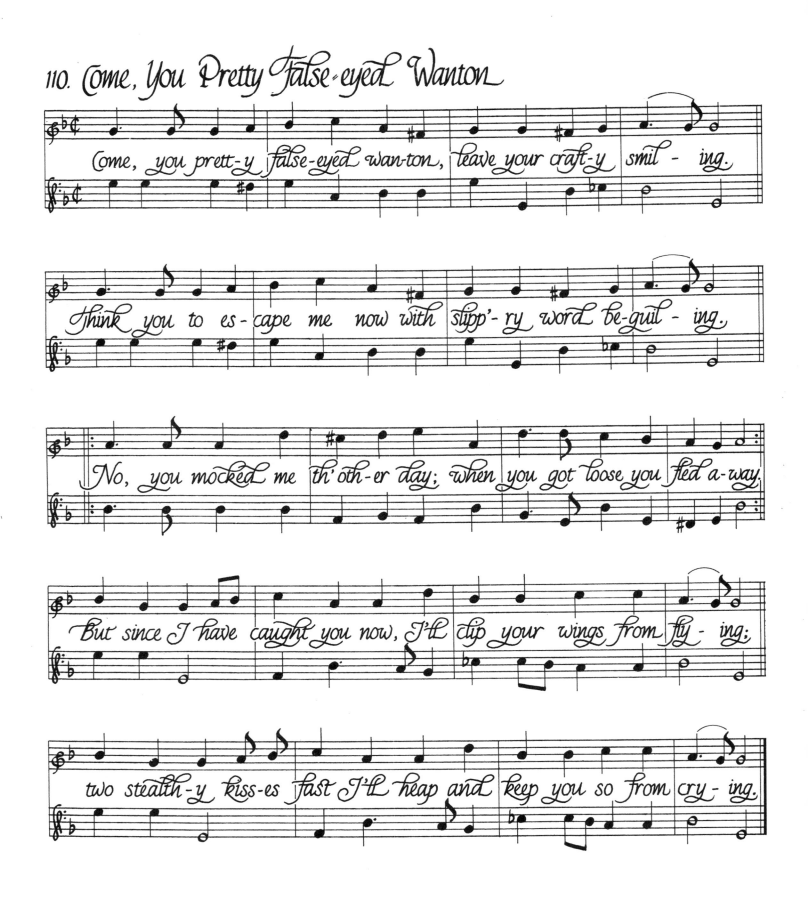

Come, you pretty false-eyed wanton, leave your crafty smiling.

Think you to escape me now with slipp'ry word beguiling.

No, you mocked me th'other day; when you got loose you fled away.

But since I have caught you now, I'll clip your wings from flying;

two stealthy kisses fast I'll heap and keep you so from crying.

111. All You Forsaken Lovers, Come

All you for-sak-en lov-ers, come and pit-y my dis-tress; I'll tell you
why; all ye be-lov-ed can pit-y me no less, for love I die.

Yet hope at last to move pit-y from hot breast, my poor heart may
find some rest which hath so long been pained to share my dis-
tress, my faith and love un-feign-ed

caused my death and they to view of all their judge-ments, which were

true, rip up my heart Oh then I [fear the world will find

thy pict-ure there.]

Analytical Notes

The analytical notes are numbered in the order of the pieces. At the beginning of each note is the original manuscript spelling of the title, followed by the foliation number of the British Museum, the facing side of any leaf being indicated with an arabic numeral, and the reverse side of the same leaf by the same numeral followed by the letter *b*. Words that have been completely or partially lost in the binding have been supplied parenthetically. The manuscript will be referred to in the notes as "Rogers." The word manuscript will be abbreviated as MS.

1. Sr Tho: ffairfax Marche, f. 2.

   Sir Thomas Fairfax, third Baron Fairfax, was born 17 January 1612. He was the leading Parliamentary general, referred to as "the man most beloved and relied upon by the rebels in the north." He was opposed to the execution of Charles I, but could do nothing to prevent it. He worked toward and was very influential in the restoration of Charles II. He was a collector of MSS and himself wrote many treatises on such varied subjects as the breeding of horses and the history of the Church to the Reformation. He also wrote a metrical version of parts of the Bible, including the Psalms, and much original verse. See Introduction, p. ix, regarding his possible ownership of the present MS.

2. Nanns Maske, f. 2b.

   This differs only slightly from the "French Almaine" by Orlando Gibbons in the Cosyn MS. A piece called "The Wooing of Nan" was a very popular stage jig of the Elizabethan era. This piece may be an adaptation or excerpt of that jig.

3. Almaygne, f. 2b.

4. The ffairest Nimphes the valleys or mountaines euer bred, & c., f. 3.

   This piece is referred to in Chappell (I, 319).* It is a dirge or funeral song. There is an instance of the tune recorded in 1634.

---

* Chappell = *The Ballad Literature and Popular Music of the Olden Time*, by William Chappell, 1859 (Dover reprint, 1965).

5. The Scots Marche, f. 3b.

6. Prince Ruperts Martch, f. 4.

   Prince Rupert was the third son of Elizabeth, Queen of Bohemia (sister of Charles I), and Frederick V, Elector Palatine. He was born 17 December 1619. A professional soldier, he came to England in 1642 to fight for the Royalist cause. As commander of the cavalry he became the foremost general in Charles's army during the Civil War. He was handsome and prepossessing and was called "the greatest beau" as well as "the greatest hero." The piece is listed in Chappell (II, 433) as being contained in Rogers, but the tunes are entirely different. Number 66 of Rogers is another setting of the present tune.

   (1) d in the MS.

7. One of ye Symphon(ies), f. 4b.

   The "symphony" seems to be a piece in the nature of a prelude or an interlude, having no definite form.

8. One of ye Symphonies, f. 5.

   See note 7. This piece is a keyboard transcription of one of the symphonies in the masque *The Triumph of Peace*, with music by William Lawes.

9. Selebrand, f. 5b.

   This is the only sarabande in the collection which follows exactly the traditional form of the sarabande. This setting was almost certainly embellished in performance.

   (1) Two crotchets in the MS.

10. When the King enioyes his owne againe, f. 5b.

    This piece is listed in Chappell (II, 434). This tune

119

seems to have been the rallying song of Royalist interests during the time of the Civil War, the Commonwealth and the Protectorate, and at the Restoration.

11. Almaygne, f. 6.

12. A Trumpett tune, f. 6b.

13. Essex last goodnight, f. 7.

Listed in Chappell (I, 174), the tune has sixteen measures with which the tune in Rogers corresponds to the first eight. The song was popular upon the death of Walter Devereux, first Earl of Essex, who died 22 September 1576. Its popularity was revived in 1601, when on 25 February Robert Devereux, second Earl of Essex and "favorite" of Elizabeth I, was executed.
(1) D in the MS.

14. Almaygne per Tho: Strengthfeild, f. 7.

15. The Corrant to y̆ last Alm(aygne) per Tho: Strengthfeild, f. 7b.

16. Ruperts Retraite, f. 7b.

On Prince Rupert, see note 6.

17. Almaygne per Tho: Strengthfeild, f. 8.

18. Corrant to y̆ former Alma(ygne) per Tho: Strengthfeild, f. 8b.

19. (Untitled), f. 8b.

This piece is not listed in the MS index (f. 1b) but is in the same hand as the other works later in the MS and was probably added at a slightly later date than the pieces surrounding it.

20. The Nightingale, f. 9.

See no. 59.

21. Corrant Bear(e), f. 9b.

The meaning of "beare" in this and subsequent titles remains unexplained. A possible, but very fanciful, explanation is that "beare" was a very common usage for barley, specifically the type with six rows of pearls, thus making reference to the notes of these pieces, all in 6/4 time, as being comparable to the six pearls of barley. But this is very farfetched.

22. Selebrand Beare, f. 9b.

See note 21 regarding the title. This piece may have been intended as a companion piece to 21.
(1) GG in the MS.

23. Corrant Beare, f. 10.

See note 21 regarding the title.

24. Almayne, f. 10.

In Christ Church MS 1113 (Oxford), this piece is ascribed to Robert Johnson.

25. Corrant, f. 10b.

26. Corrant Beare, f. 11.

See note 21 regarding the title.
(1) e' in the MS.

27. Corrant Beare, f. 11.

See note 21 regarding the title.
(1) Crotchet in the MS; (2) crotchets in the MS; (3) D in the MS; (4) A in the MS; (5) G in the MS; (6) F in the MS.

28–39. *The Battaile, ff. 11b–18.*

This suite is perhaps the best known of the earliest attempts at programmatic music for the keyboard. Its first appearance is in *My Ladye Nevells Booke* (1591), in which it is thought to have been copied directly from the autograph of its composer, William Byrd. Apart from the present collection, it is found also in Paris Conservatoire MS 18546 (containing two pieces more than Nevell: a "Morris" and "Ye Souldiers Dance") and, in an incomplete version, in Christ Church MS 431. Rogers contains one more piece than Nevell, "The Burying of the Dead." Immediately following the suite in Rogers, there is a piece entitled "The Soldiers' Delight," which is a more elaborate setting of "Ye Souldiers Dance" found in the Paris Conservatoire MS. It is probable, because of the vast discrepancy between these two settings, that these pieces are not the work of Byrd but rather anonymous settings of a familiar tune appended because of the relationship of the subject matter. The extra piece in Rogers, "The Burying of the Dead," has a more fortunate pedigree in that it is contained almost exactly in a piece by Byrd, "A Medley," found in *The Fitzwilliam Virginal Book* (II, 220). The Nevell MS also contains, immediately prior to the suite, a piece not contained in any of the other versions, entitled "The Marche before the Battell," which is more commonly referred to as "My Lord of Oxenford's Maske" or "The Earle of Oxfords Marche" (see *Fitzwilliam Virginal Book* II, 402). It is interesting to note that there is a one-line fragment (f. 31) in the MS which corresponds exactly to the first phrase of this march.

28. The Souldiars summons, f. 11b.

29. The Martch of ffoote, f. 12.

(1) BB, D, F in the MS; (2) G in the MS; (3) AA, E, A in the MS.

30. (The) Martch (of) horse, ff. 12–12b.

31. The Trumpetts, ff. 12b–13.

32. The Irish Martch, ff. 13b–14.

33. Bagpipes, ff. 14–14b.
(1) g in the MS; (2) F in the MS.

34. The Drum̃ and fflute, ff. 14b–16.

The scribe of the MS saved time and ink by not writing out each chord for the left hand. Instead he wrote only the bass note and indicated the unchanging harmony with ciphers at the end of each line.
(1) g', f' in the MS. This measure contains seven beats in the right hand as opposed to the correct six. This reading is on the authority of the Nevell MS.

35. The Martch (to) ẙ ffight, ff. 16–16b.

While this and the following two pieces are divided in the MS, it is suggested that they be played without interruption.

(1) d in the MS; (2) d in the MS; (3) A in the MS.

36. Tarra-tantarra, f. 17.

37. (The) Battell Joyned, ff. 17–17b.

38. Retrait, f. 17b.

39. The Buriing of the dead, f. 18.

This piece bears the inscription at the end: "The end of the Battell."

40. The Souldiers delight, f. 18b.

See note 28–39.
(1) EE in the MS.

41. Corrant, f. 19.

42. Selebrand, f. 19.

Possibly intended as a companion piece to 41.

43. A Maske, f. 19b.

44. Corrant, f. 20.

45. Selebrand, f. 20.

Possibly intended as a companion piece to 44.

46. Ly still my Deare, ff. 20b–21.

Part of the lyric occurs in Chappell (I, 173) to a tune entirely different from the present example, being "Loth to Depart," a popular tune of the time (see *Fitzwilliam Virginal Book* II, 317). The lyrics of these two settings are obviously from the same poem although they are not word perfect. The words in Dryden's *Miscellany Poems* are attributed to "Mr. J(ohn) Donne." *The Oxford Book of English Verse* entitles it "Daybreak."

Ly still my Deare, why dost thou rise; / the light that shines, comes from thine eyes: / the day breakes not, it is my heart; / to think that thou and I must part: / Oh stay, Oh stay, Oh stay or else my ioyes must dye. / & perish in their infancie.

47. The Chestnut, f. 21.

(1) d' in the MS.

48. Cloris sight, ff. 21b–22.

The Catalogue of Manuscript Music in the British Museum, volume III, states that this piece is "adapted from R. Balls."

Cloris sight, and songe, & wept; / sighing songe, & singing slept: / and wakes; sighes, singes, & weepes againe; / for Amintas, Oh Amintas that was slaine: / Oh, Oh had yoᵘ seene his face (quoth shee) / how sweet, how full of maiesty; / & there shee stop't: and thus shee cry'd / amintas, Amintas; and so shee dy'd.

49. Now ẙ springe is comne, ff. 22b–23.

The tune of this piece is in Chappell (II, 463) as "Christmas's Lamentation" and the words in the Roxburghe collection,* entitled "A Lover's desire for his best beloved; or Come away, come away, and do not stay. To an excellent new Court tune." It was probably during the reigns of Elizabeth I and James I that the tune was also popular as "Christmas's Lamentation."

Now ẙ springe is comne, / turne to thy Loue, to thy loue, to thy loue, / to thy Loue make noe delay: / heare I will fill thy lap full of flowers; / and Couer thee with shadie Bowers, / come away; come away, come away and do not stay.

50. Ôh Iesu meeke, f. 23.

Ôh Iesu meeke, Ô Iesu sweete; / Ô Iesu saviour mine: / most gratious Iesu to my call; / thy gratious eares incline.

51. Corrant, f. 23b.

52. Corrant, f. 24.

53. Maske, f. 24b.

54. Corrant, f. 25.

(1) GG in the MS.

55. Almaygne, f. 25b.

(1) d♯ in the MS.

56. Lupus Ayre, f. 26.

"Lupus" may very well refer to the composer, Thomas Lupo.

(1) C in the MS; (2) minim in the MS; (3) crotchet in the MS; (4) dotted minim in the MS.

57. Could thine incomparable eye, ff. 26b–27.

Could thine incomparable eye: / Beame forth, beame forth, beame forth, such Amability: / then has my winning pen the art, my winning pen the Art; / To steare, to steare Affection, and to Charme yoʳ hart.

58. Almaygne: Mʳ Johnson, ff. 27b–28b.

This piece appears as an "Alman" and "Italian Ground" in various MSS in which it is attributed to Orlando Gibbons.

(1) EE, BB in the MS; (2) BB in the MS; (3) DD in the MS; (4) E in the MS.

59. Mock-Nightingale, f. 29.

See no. 20.
(1) Minim in the MS.

60. What if the King should come to ẙ City, f. 29b.

(1) A in the MS.

61. The Kings Complaint, f. 30.

This piece is listed in Chappell (II, 439). It also appears in the first edition (1650) of John Playford's *The Dancing Master*, in which it is entitled "Fain I would if I could." A ballad from the *King's Pamphlets* (23 April, 1649) is entitled "A Coffin for King Charles: A Crown for Cromwell: A Pit for the People" and it is noted that

---

* *Roxburghe Ballads*, ed. by William Chappell and J. W. Ebsworth, 1871–1899.

121

"you may sing this to the tune of 'Fain I Would.'"
This is probably the version from which the present
piece is taken. The resemblance of the tunes is apparent
but by no means exact. There is a slight chance that this
piece was intended as a companion piece to 60, their
titles seeming to complement one another.

62. Almaygne, f. 30b.

(1) G in the MS.

63. Corrant, f. 30b.

This piece may have been intended as a companion piece
to 62.

64. Selebrand, f. 31.

65. My Delyght, f. 31b.

66. A Scotts Tuen, f. 32 (inverted).

This is another setting of no. 6.

(1) BB in the MS.

67. An Irish Toy, f. 32b (inverted).

The numbers above the notes on the treble staff are
indications of fingering from the MS. It is interesting to
note support of that theory of harpsichord technique
which suggests that repeated notes of the same pitch
should not be played by the same finger.

(1) These four measures (5, 6, 9, 10) stand as
printed in the MS, but it is probable that all note
values should be doubled.

68. Allmayne, f. 32b (inverted).

(1) Minim AA in the MS; (2) g, b, d' in the MS;
(3) F in the MS; (4) FF in the MS.

69. The spaynard, f. 33 (inverted).

70. (Untitled), f. 33 (inverted).

(1) B in the MS.

71. Selabrand, f. 34 (inverted).

72. The ffinex, f. 34–33b (inverted).

(1) E in the MS.

73. The faithfull Brothers, f. 34b (inverted).

Listed in Chappell (I, 157). A copy of this tune, with
lyrics evidently about Elizabeth I, is found in a MS of
about the year 1600. The tunes have an obvious resemblance but are not exact.

(1) F in the MS.

74. A Corant, f. 34b (inverted).

(1) e' in the MS; (2) editorial addition: A not included
in the MS; (3) E in the MS; (4) D, F in the MS;
(5) C in the MS; (6) the middle voice in this
measure incorrectly reads as having the following four
beats: crotchet F, minim G, crotchet B (here
eliminated); (7) BBB in the MS.

The two pieces following are of special interest. They
are representative of the popular vocal dialogue pieces
that flourished at the time in the form of ballads, broad-
sides and jigs.

75. This soldier loues, ff. 36–35b (inverted).

This piece has at the end the composer's name, "M^r
Balles."

This soldier loues and ffaine would dye to win, / shall hee
goo in, No tis to ffowle a sinn, / he must nott come abourd,
I dare nott row, / stormes of disspaire and guilty bloud
will blowe: / shall time release him say: o no, o no, / nor
time nor death can alter us nor prayers: / my boate is
Destany, and who then Dares, / but those apointed com
abourd liue still / and loue by resone mortall nott by will.
/ and when thy ni^{gt} shall close up thine eies: / (Choris) Then
com aboord and passe tell then bee wise: Tell then bee
wisse.

76. Carron o carron, ff. 37–36b (inverted).

Dialogues between a lover and Charon, the ferryman to
the Underworld, were very common in many forms.

Carron o carron, / thou wafter off the soules to blis or
baine: / who calles the ferriman off hell: Com neare / and
say who liues in Joy and who in feare: / Those y^t dye well
— etearnall Joies shall follow: / those that dye Ill There
owne foule fate shall ffwollow: / shall thy blacke barke
those guilty spirrits stow / that kills themselues ffor loue:
o no o no: / my cordage crakes when such foule sins are
neare: / No winde blowes faier nor I myselfe can steare: /
what spirrits pas an in Eliziam Raigne: / Those gentell
soulls y^t are beloued againe:

77. A horne pipe, ff. 37b–38.

The scribe of this piece apparently started a fourth
too low and could not completely erase his mistake,
so there seem to be incorrect harmonies in the first
two measures.

78. Almaygne, f. 39b.

79. Corrant per Tho: Strengthfeild, f. 40.

This piece was probably intended as a companion piece
to 78.

80. Selebrand, f. 40.

81. Almaine, f. 40b (inverted).

This piece is a courant in form rather than an allemande.

82. Corant, f. 40b (inverted).

This piece seems to be incomplete in the MS, stopping
abruptly at the end of measure 9. Since measure 9 is a
repetition of measure 5, and cipher notes at the end of
the measure indicate that measure 10 would have begun
on the same notes as measure 6, the latter has been used
(with the bass line raised an octave as indicated by the
cipher notes) to complete the piece at a point of logical
cadence.

(1) G in the MS; (2) F in the MS.

83. Almaygne, f. 41 (inverted).

(1) The dot is incorrectly placed after the g in the MS.

84. I wish noe more, f. 41b.

The Catalogue of Manuscript Music in the British Museum,
volume III, notes that this piece is "usually attributed
to Nic. Laniere, but to 'Mr. Warner' in Playford's

Select Ayres'' (1659). No. 100 is another setting of this piece.

(1) AA in the MS; (2) C in the MS.

> I wish noe more thou should'st loue mee / my joyes are ffull in louing thee / my hart's too narrow to containe / my blisse if thou should'st loue againe

85. (Untitled), f. 42.

This piece is not listed in the MS table of contents.

86. Selebrand, T: S:, f. 42.

(1) Minim EE in the MS.

87. Loue is strange, f. 42b.

88. Almaygne Mercure, f. 43.

New York Public Library Drexel MS 5611 contains five pieces which list the composer as ''Mercure.'' This use of one name is unusual in that MS where normally two names are given and/or ''Mister'' or ''Monsieur'' is used. The pieces in the Drexel MS are of a complexity similar to that of this one, which is unusual in the Rogers MS. See note 91.

89. Glory of yᵉ North, f. 43b.

This piece is listed in Chappell (II, 442).

90. Almaine, f. 44.

This piece is untitled in the text of the MS but is listed as quoted above in the table of contents (f. 1b).

(1) f in the MS.

91. Merceur, f. 44.

In the MS, the title is preceded by the antique planetary symbol ☿ for Mercury, the Evening Star. See note 88.

(1) B in the MS.

92. Corrant, f. 44b.

93. Corrant, f. 44b.

94. Phill: Porters Lamentation, f. 45.

This piece is listed in Chappell (II, 614) and is also found in the Skene MSS (1630 or 1640).

Voycall Lessons, ff. 59b–46b (inverted).

95. Psalme 42, f. 59b (inverted).

This piece is arranged from an anthem for three voices by William Lawes (Psalm 42, verses 1–2).

> Lord as the hart Imbost with heate. / brayes affter the coole reuelott: / so sighes my soule ffor the, / my soule Thirsts for the liueing god: / when shall I enter his abode, / and there his beauty see:

96. Must your faire, f. 59 (inverted).

(1) Crotchet C and quaver D, quaver E in MS.

> must your faire inflaming eye, / make a world in loue as I: / all consenting, no repenting: / as you will to liue or dye
>
> 2 your ffaire lookes and rare deserts, / keeps in awe my yealding hart, / yett by praying and obeying, / I doe hope to bare a part.
>
> 3 yett though I should plainly see, / your disdaine would

murder me, / Twould not fright me, but delight me / That I might your marter bee.

97. Since tis my Fate, f. 58b (inverted).

(1) F# in the MS; (2) E in the MS; (3) a continuo notation (see page xxii).

> Since tis my fate to bee thy slaue, / vnder such pitty thou wouldst craue: / iff twere my fortune soe to bee, / to him that courts his Desstany.

98. No flattring pellow, ff. 58–57b (inverted).

This piece has the name of the composer, ''Mʳ Willson,'' at the end.

> No flattring pellow Downny beed: / vpon yᵉ ffattall mos and willow, / I lay my much tormented head, / and sight and weep, / vntell I keepe / Just passes with my sorrow: / Thus hardly can so sad a man / distinguish night from morrow:
>
> My Day is clouded and my nights, / in mesty discontented shrouded / and left quitt loss to all delight / Saue but my crime, / I hould with time, / no recking Booke nor Tally, / The ffountains keepe, the teares I weepe, / my graue lies in the vally.

99. Baloo my boy, ff. 57–56b (inverted).

Listed as an anonymous lyric of the sixteenth century by *The Oxford Book of English Verse*, in which the first three verses compare very closely. The present fourth verse is not recorded in *The Oxford Book*, although four others not listed in Rogers are. There is the initial ''W.'' at the end of the piece in Rogers, which probably indicates authorship by William Lawes.

(1) Possibly these notes D, D should read BB♭, BB♭ to parallel measure 12; (2) possibly should be a D.

> Baloo my boy lye still and sleepe, / itt grieues me sore To see the weepe: / wouldst thou bee quiet ist be as glade. / Thy morninge, makes my sorrow sad: / Lie still my boy, thy mothers Joy, / Thy father coulde mee great anoy: / Laloo, Baloo, laloo, laloo, laloo, laloo, laloo, / Baloo, baloo, Baloo, baloo; / Baloo, Baloo.
>
> 2 When he began to court my loue, / and with his sug'rd words did moue / His flattering face and faigned cheare, / To mee that tyme did not apeare. / But now I see, that cruell hee / cares nether for my boy, nor mee. / Baloo baloo
>
> 3 But thou my Darlinge. sleepe a while, / and when thou wakest sweetlye smile, / yet smile not as thy father did / to cusen mads, nay god forbid / But yett i feare that thou willt heare / Thy fathers face and hart still beare / Baloo //://://:
>
> 4 Now by my greifs I vow and sweare / the and all others to forbeare / I'lle neuer kisse nor cull nor clapp / But lull my youngling in my lapp, / cease hart to moane, leaue of to groane, / and sleepe securelye hart alone / Baloo //://://:

100. Ile wish no more, f. 56 (inverted).

See note 84 regarding this song.

> Ile wish no more, thou shouldst loue me, / my Joyes are full in louing the: / my harts to narrow, too Contayne, / my bliss iff thou shouldst loue againe:

2 Thy scornes may wound me but my fate / ledes me to loue and the to hate / yett must I loue whilst I haue breth / for nott to loue, weare worse then Death.

3 Then shall I sue for scorne or grace / a lingring life or Death imbrace, / Since on off theise I needs must try / loue mee but once and lett mee Dye.

101. Deerest loue, f. 55b (inverted).

Deerest loue I doo not goe, / for weariness of the, / or that all the world can showe, / a fitter loue for me : / But since that I must dye att last, / tis best to vse my selfe in Jeast, / Thus by fained Death to Die :

102. No noe I tell ẙ no, ff. 55–54b (inverted).

This piece has the name of the composer, "Mʳ John Willson," at the end.

no noe I tell ẙ no, / though ffrom thee I must goe, / yett my heart sayes nott soe : / Itt swears by stellas eyes, / by whose Dalling surprise, itt in loues fetters lies : / Itt sware by those roses and lylles soe whitt / and thoss rubies so bright, / neire to part, neire to partt, ffrom my Deare, Deare delight.

2 Itt sweares by that warme snow in thy bosome below, / wher blind loue hids his bow, / And by those milke whit hands that dispence Cupeds bands, / and the quiuer commandes, / And lett that forme deuine, and thoss smale nembell feet, / in loue ware too too flet / nere to part, nere to part stella bright stella sweet.

3 By our true loue itt swares, by our hopes, by our ffeares, / by our sad parting tares, / And by this mellting kisse, ffull off greife, full off blisse, / by this too and by this / And by this last imbrace and this cruell adew, / and by high heauen to / Neare to change, neare to change, stellas loue for a new.

103. O that myne eyes, ff. 54–53b (inverted).

The name of the composer, "Tho. Breuer," is at the end of this piece.

(1) g′ in the MS ; (2) f′ in the MS.

Ø That myne eyes could melt into a flod / ẙ I might plung in teares for the : / as thou didst swim in blod / to ransom mee, / Ø That this fleshly limbeck would begine / to drop, and drop a teare for euery sine :

2 See how his bloude, bedabled Armes are spread, / To entetayne deaths welcome bands. / Behould his bowing head / his bleeding hands. / His oft repeated strpes his wounded side / harke how hee grooned, remember how hee dyde.

3 The verye Heauenes put weedes of sable on, / The verie rockes asunder rent. / And yett this heart that ston / will not relent, / Hard harted man for onely man denyde, / To mourne for him, for whome hee only dyde.

104. Yes I could loue, ff. 53–52b (inverted).

The name of the composer, "Tho. Brewer," is at the end of this piece.

Yes I could loue, could I but finde / a mʳⁱˢ fitting to my minde : / who neither pride, nor gould could moue, / to by hir Beautie, sell hir loue, / weare neate yett care not to be fine, / and loue me ffor myselfe not myne : / nott lady Proude, nor Cetty coy, / but ffull off freedome, full off Joy :

nott wise enough to rule a state, / nor foole enough to bee

laught att. / nott childeish young nor Beldom old, / nott fyrie hott nor Isey coulde, Nott richly proude nor Basely poore / nott chast yett no reeputed whore / If shuch a on I chanse to finde, / I haue a mˢᵗ, to my mynde.

105. Lett god the god of Battaile Rize, f. 52 (inverted).

This piece is arranged from an anthem for three voices by William Lawes (Psalm 68, verses 1–2).

Lett god the god of Battaile Rize. / and scatter his proud Enemies, / Ô Lett them flee before his face, / Like smoak wᶜʰ driuing tempests Chase, / as wax dissoues with scorching fire, / So perish in his burning Ire.

106. Sing to the king of kings, f. 51b (inverted).

This piece is arranged from an anthem for three voices by William Lawes (Psalm 98, verse 1). The complete three-part setting is quoted in Burney's *History* (II, 319).*

Sing to the king of kings / sing in vnusuall Layes. / that hath wrought wondros things. / his Conquest Crownd wᵗʰ praise, / whose Armes alone & sacred hands, their Impious bands haue over throwne, there : // :

107. Psalme 39. verse 12, ff. 50b–51 (inverted).

This piece has at the end the initials, "W : L.," indicating authorship by William Lawes (Psalm 39, verses 11–13).

When man ffor sinne Thy Judgments feeles, / Just as a moth / consumes a cloth : / his beauty fades, in strength he reeles : / man is all vanity : all uanity and ffull off ills : / Ø spare me lord : : // : lord a while. / ẙ I may gaine some strengt, : // : beefore I Die.
But lord vnto my praiers draw neare. / lend gratious eares / and see my teares / Øn earth I am a soiourner / As all my ffathers were, / Ø spare me lord : : // :

108. I preethe sweete, ff. 50–49b (inverted).

The composer's name, "Mʳ Hen. Lawes," is at the end of this piece. It is interesting here to note that in the last lines of this song, the words "good" and "sweet" and "faire" (which agree with a copy in *Select Ayres and Dialogues*, 1669) have been crossed out and replaced by the words "wilde" and "naught" and "failce," which have been given in the transcription. Correlating this with the lovesick poetic fragment (60b; see Introduction, p. xv), one begins to feel that perhaps the lady in question at some point was thwarted in her love.

I preethe sweete to mee be kind : / Delight not so in scoring : / I sue for loue. Ø lett me ffind / some pleasure midst my mourning : / what Thought to you I vassall bee, / lett me my right inhirreitt, / send backe the hart I gaue to the. / Since thine itt can not merritt : / So I shall to the worlde Declare, / how wilde (good) how naught (sweet) and failce (faire) you are.

109. fyer : // :, ff. 49–48b (inverted).

This setting is by Nicholas Laniere. The lyrics are ascribed to Thomas Campian, who published the first setting of them in *The Third Booke of Ayres* (1617). The words of both settings are almost identical.

---

* *A General History of Music*, by Charles Burney, 1776–1789 (1935 edition reprinted by Dover, 1957.)

fyer: //: / loe here I burne in such Desire: / ỹ all ỹ teares, that I can straine, / out off myne emptie loue sick Braine: / can nott alay my scorchinge paine: Com Humber Trent: and siluer Thames. / Dread ocean hast, with all thy streames: / And iff you cannott quench my fyer, / Ø Drowne both mee and my desire:

ffyer fier: / Ther is noe Hell to my desire, / see all the ryuers backward fly, / And the ocean doth his ayde deny, / for feare my heate should drinke them dry / Come heauenly showers then powringe Downe, / Come you that once, the world did Drowne. / som then you spard, but now saue all, / Thatt elce might burne, and with mee fall

110. Come you pritty, f. 48 (inverted).

This piece is by Thomas Campian.

Come you pritty false eyd wanton / leaue your Craftie smiling / thinke you To escape me now / with slipry word beeguiling / no you mocke me th'other day / when you got loos you fled away / bout since I haue caughtt you now / Ile Clip your wings from flying / two shelthy kisses fast Ile heape / and kepe you sae from Crying.

111. All you forsaken louers, f. 47 (inverted).

(1) e♭′ in the MS; (2) B♮ in the MS.

All you forsaken louers Come & pitty my distrese / Ill tell you why / all yee beloued can pitty mee no lesse for loue I dye / yet hope at last to moue pitty from hot brist / my p°ore harte may find some rest / wᶜʰ hath so long beène painᵉd / to sher my distriss my faith and loue unfained.

112. Think not deare, f. 46b (inverted).

This piece is incomplete in the MS, but the remainder of the text, entitled "Secresie Protested," by Thomas Carew, is supplied from two separate settings by William and Henry Lawes. This setting does not seem to be a fragment of either of these pieces.

Thinke not deare loue that Ill reyeale / the houres of plesure wee tow steale / no eye shale see nor yet the sun / discry what thee & I haue done. / The God of loue himselfe whose dart / did first pierce mine & next thy hart / He shale not know yᵗ wee can tell / what sweets in stolne embracements dwᵉll / Onely this means may find it out: / if when I dy Phisitians doubt / what Cayst my death & thay to uiew / of all thier iudgemᵗˢ wᶜʰ were true / rip vp my hart oh then I (end MS) feare / the Worlde will fynde thy Picture there.